A MAP OF THE LOST WORLD

PITT POETRY SERIES

Ed Ochester, Editor

A Map of the Lost World

RICK HILLES

University of Pittsburgh Press

Published by the University of Pittsburgh Press, Pittsburgh, Pa., 15260
Copyright © 2012, Rick Hilles
All rights reserved
Manufactured in the United States of America
Printed on acid-free paper
10 9 8 7 6 5 4 3 2 1
ISBN 13: 978-0-8229-6182-6
ISBN 10: 0-8229-6182-2

For Nancy

And in loving memory of:
Dr. Thaddeus Stabholz
(October 16, 1917–March 22, 2009)
childhood physician & beloved lifelong friend
&
Lucile M. Kelley
(December 22, 1915–November 19, 2010)
my maternal grandmother, a second mother

NTRAL ARKANSAS LIBRARY SYSTEM
TLE ROCK PUBLIC LIBRARY
0 ROCK STREET
TLE ROCK, ARKANSAS 72201

CONTENTS

The sorry verities!
Yet in excess, continual,
There is a cure for sorrow.

Permit that if as a ghost I come
Among the people burning in me still.

—Wallace Stevens, "The Weeping Burgher"

A MAP OF THE LOST WORLD

Missoula Eclipse

Believe the couple who have finished their picnic/and
make wet love in the grass. . . . Believe in milestones,
the day/you left home forever and the cold open way/a
world would not let you come in.
—(Part of the inscription on Richard Hugo's headstone in
Missoula, MT, from his poem, "Glen Uig.")

If I could live again as just one thing
it would be this early autumn wind
as it cartwheels the rooftops and avenues
of the Pacific Northwest; the way the air
of orchards vaulted in the mind of Keats
as he brimmed over with his last Odes
dreaming of the mouths his final words
would touch and kiss through any darkness

like a shooting star; the way a starry-eyed
stranger once blew smoke into the night
before offering me her cigarette outside
the 92nd Street Y, where I'd just given
a reading, so that I didn't even notice
sad-faced Jim Wright in a patch of leaves.
And there we were again, Jim weeping
and breathless to tell me he'd stopped drinking

and was in love; and, in a voice reserved
for children (and the very lost), told me
he had cancer. I wish we had hightailed it
then into my dream of Rome, the dream
where we are laughing at our dumb luck
and near giddy as we exit the gilded portal
and enter a day too bright to see the Spanish steps,
where, for us, apparently, it is always noon;

I always wanted to take Jim to Rome—
to see the black ink of cuttlefish

and shadows blue the edges of his grin
even if we were just to stand penniless and eye
the sparkling wishes tossed into fountains,
one whose water surrounds a sculpted hull
of a boat that's lost its mast, held in a state
of perpetual sinking as Jim points to the flat

where John Keats died, his friend Severn
at his side, drawing him over and over—
even after his last torment; Jim tells me
about the dream he's having lately
in which Keats appears, practically
flying up and down the Spanish Steps
in in-line blades; Jim wants so badly
to grab the frilly garment of the white-

shirted Romantic, who now is naked
to the waist and in black spandex,
in death forever beautiful and ridiculous,
but Jim's afraid to wake us from the dream.
Still, there's a melody under Keats's breath.
It might be from Handel's *Water Music*
or just the syncopated rhythms of the boat
we ride, Our Fountain of the Sinking Ship.

Oh, to be so close to the poet we love
who died at half our age not knowing
what he would become for so many of us,
understandably, makes us a little insane.
Jim asks if I know what it all means
and then he's coming at me like Sonny Liston,
as if the only way affection can be shown
between men like us is with an open fist.

And, forgetting a moment that I am
not even the merest breeze in your living hair,
and that a boneyard in Missoula, Montana,
negates this vision, just now to my dead friend
I'm real as any man who's loved his life,
and, stunned by it, tries to face what he can't take,
when the trees of Rome rattle their silver leaves,
and Jim picks me up, like nothing, in his arms.

I

Nights & Days of 2007: Autumn

For James Merrill and with thanks to the Stonington
Village Improvement Association

1.

Stonington harbor: now a pulsating roofside
Shingled in mirrors, now paparazzi flashes,
Or a shimmying rhinestone dress so alluring
One forgets what lies beyond this brightness.
Inscrutable portents of another early September:
A "loonie" is now more stable than the dollar;
In a German spa town miles of SS secrets
Still elude public scrutiny—now sixty-plus years.

(How long it takes to unfurl one scroll of History.)
Walls glistening like sliced peaches in late daylight
Turn four billowy white curtains orange-pink,
A prank of bed-sheet apparitions, at the table
Where our late host JM entertained spirits
Via a Ouija board, and we now take our seats.

2.

A fratboy would-be sideshow freak who dangles
A black salamander down his throat dares us
To swim a lake. Halfway, I see my grave: my arms
Rubbery and useless, my feet disoriented fish.
My friend Jason, the stronger swimmer, talks me
Onto my back describing the patterns of clouds.
His calming voice keeping me in tow blindly
As we gradually span the vast sparkling surface.

Some bonds don't easily break. He writes: from Papua
New Guinea; atop Mt. Fuji; of a girlfriend in Honolulu
Who becomes his wife by Anchorage. Then nothing.
Then I find this Internet headline: "Hawaiian artist
And writer-husband die in Alaska." Lucy—
In a Coast Guard chopper. Divers never find Jason.

3.

That night I drizzle four amber tears of rum
On the gumline of a willowware cup
Making sure to spread the spirit lubricant
Thoroughly along the cracked bone-white cranium
Before setting it mouth down on a Ouija board
Whose ghost-galleon absinthe-glow rides the dark.
Our first disembodied parlor guest arrives:
My lost college friend, Jason Greer.

Neither asks who stopped corresponding.
First, the letters come in rapid fire.
Then the teacup chills. Needles of hypothermia
As if Jason's drowning—but to us this time.
I rub my hands together to warm them then clasp
The cup harder before calling it a night.

4.

In the nights and days to come, Jason describes:
(1.) A love beyond our understanding;
How like the morning news he "wakes to it."
(2.) A novel, undone—"thinly disguised
Autobiography" he's still unsure how to finish;
Then he asks for news of the living.
I wonder if he knows? His parents named
An artist foundation for Lucy and him.

I start to say this when the fist-sized crystal amulet
Hanging by a black string flashes a four-leaf clover
Of brightness that spins disco prismatic light
Till the string snaps, the amulet crashes down,
Leaving the milk glass in six uneven pie slices,
New cracks in all we know silence the willowware.

5.

Maybe some things aren't meant to span the space
Between the dead and living. Days pass in which
The six uneven cream pie slices of milk glass
Seem an underworld entrance closed for repairs.
No word from Jason, and a dark static now pervades
The House from within: our new party animal
Downstairs neighbors won't give us any rest;
We contemplate cutting short our time here

When we sense a new tremor stirring in the willowware.
It's Halloween night—and "on the line" is JM.
Even in death, the legendary host wants to help us.
He proposes "an intervention"—a benign haunting
Of our oblivious housemates. "Just a talking to," he says.
In his presence even the shadows seem to wink.

6.

All Saints'. A silence in the floorboards
Sprouts a tree whose invisibly thickening roots
Spread and stretch to fill what had been noise
With something like a cat purring at our ears.
No use explaining. We simply spread
More rum along the willowware. Say Thanks.
Our next spirit guide arrives: *Stefan Celichówski*—
Nineteen when Poland capitulates to the Nazis.

Five days later, he escapes a prison for officers
To join *"a guerrilla unit of the Underground Army."*
The candle flickers. Now the room seems more like
A cavernous mine shaft that runs between two worlds.
Our hearts are racing now as he leads us along
Like resistance fighters through the sewers of Warsaw.

7.

The night I first heard Stefan's name, he died.
September. My first Sunday in Stonington.
Our new friends promised to introduce us
Not knowing that earlier that day he passed away.
The candles make strange shadows of the willowware;
Another wading pool opens in the cracked milk glass.
Our conversation with Stefan hinges on an idea,
The Old Testament notion—that to kill a man

Is to kill an entire generation. And from the Talmud:
"To save one life is as if one saved the entire world."
April '45. Days to the Liberation. Stefan
Leads four men through heavily patrolled SS lines
To tell General Patton, and Patton only, of a battalion,
Poland's last "ready to fight": 1000 STRONGK.

8.

November rains, then robin eggshell sky.
The last orange monarch of the season glides by
The sun-blistered rooftop chair where I write.
Last night, only the tapers wavered. Our fingers
Settled on the willowware then skated blindly
On the glow-in-the-dark board, echo-locating
A message spelled-out by, if not with, our hands.
"My generation was devoured by History."

That two decade-long window between the wars.
Poland's first self-rule in a century and a half.
Think of a boy listening to opera in Warsaw.
The aria hides somewhere the boy can't go.
The aria escapes the ruins of crematoria.
The aria conjures the lost boy now in you.

9.

"What happens in Merrill's House? Anything weird?"
Friends ask. "Not really," I say. Which is mostly true.
Though the paranormal manifests in small things
Misplaced, too easily ascribed to forgetfulness,
Or highbrow pranks: the almost imperceptible
Bach sonatas emanating mysteriously some nights
From the lonely, untuned concert Steinway upstairs.
But on the anniversary of 9-11, our first week here,

I froze on footage of the Twin Towers falling again.
How to explain the next sensation? Of a delicate
Arm-like wreath laid around my shoulders?
Fine as the motes of old skin tumbling in sunlight,
The blizzard of the past lit up in rooms like shooting stars
Swirling constellations. All of which we are.

10.

Last week, the final signatories (France and Greece)
Signed the treaty thereby opening the archives
At Bad Arolsen, Germany, to the public.
May we live long enough to learn what we can stomach
Of the dark secrets of last century long buried
In that German spa town and what they may tell us
Of our own time. First snows of mid-December.
Winds pounding the windows of our borrowed sanctuary.

Two weeks—all we have left in Stonington.
Our work here, such as it is, will soon be done.
What we take with us, in part, is what we leave
Behind, what we imbue any space we really inhabit
And fill with our anxious hope. Uncertainty.
Beginning with the love that brought us here.

II

The Red Scarf & the Black Briefcase

Faut se débrouiller: First, you have to know
how to help yourself, to cleave your own path
out of the nightmare. That's how you survived,
if you survived. *Faut se débrouiller*. Back then,
it might mean anything: knowing how to procure,
even falsify, valid documents; knowing when
and how to offer a bribe.
                                        Faut se débrouiller. Find
what will help you—even if, as yet, it doesn't exist.

What would you have called us? *Enemy combatants?*
"Ressortissants allemands" they called us ("citizens of
Germany"), although Germany had already rescinded
our citizenship. We were citizens of no country
—exiles, *apatrides, émigrés*. The music of French
curdling in our mouths gave us away—the despised
accent boche betrayed us as German. Gone were
the distinctions—Fascist, anti-Fascist. All Germans
after the occupation were *sales boches* ("vile expletives").

Still, it was easier to survive in Provence than Berlin.
Though the South remained, "technically," unoccupied,
French police arrested and deported many emigrants.
Yet those left by the nights and days of 1941 knew summer
well into late autumn in the small fishing town of Cassis.
Days we would lie on the hot sand or hike a *calanque*
out to *les roches blanches*, the white cliffs chiseled by salt,
wind, water, light, and time—so peaceful and solitary.
Often I'd float on my back for hours, having discovered

the buoyancy of salt water, how it lessened my appetite,
the weakness in my extremities. I imagined the sun,
its constancy, evaporating each unmet need. One day,

swimming in a secluded spot off Port Miou, I returned
to find everything stolen, even my bathing suit—catastrophe!—
now how would I get home? Luckily, I'd wrapped
a red Provençal scarf around my head, and out of it
I improvised a little something that in a decade or so
I'd hear an American girl call "a bikini."

༈

Faut se débrouiller. For some, this meant collaborating.
Apatrides like us focused on not getting caught, knowing
the right time to disappear. For me it was February 1933—
just after the election—Brownshirt attacks on known
anti-Fascists rising, a friend said: "They have their eyes
on you!" Then I had to disappear. My first luck came
in the form of two sisters: the widowed Frau Schulz
and Fräulein Gust, members of the workers' chorus
but unknowns. They owned a candy shop on *Gubener
Strasse* (specializing in dark chocolate and marzipan).

The exquisitely articulate Frau Schulz advised me
to use the secret entrance no more than once a day,
and only after having made sure the coast was clear.
Which meant casing my place from a sympathizer's
house across the street. In a pinch, I could always enter
through the candy shop. The smells of Frau Schulz
sweetening crushed almonds or Fräulein Gust's
endless experiments in dark chocolate saturated
the air, even entering the chambers of my dream-life.
Could I have possibly invented a better hiding place?

༈

Despite all that happened, and was to come,
for long moments one could almost forget about

the war. Sometimes it seemed the candy shop
conspired to hasten this sensation, whole daydreams
of fresh chocolate wafting into my living room!
I kept few essentials: some books, leaflets, a small
typewriter (already considered an instrument of
"high treason"). Finally, I smuggled in my gramophone
along with an armful of sleeveless 78s. The spinster
sisters in their caution permitted me but one regular
visitor—my girlfriend Lucie—who liked to announce
her arrival with a few choice notes emanating from
the gramophone, the bemused yawning flower of
its fat mouth. As always, the first song came from
Die Dreigroschenoper. Her favorite number arrived
in the voice of Lotte Lenya singing, "Pirate Jenny."

You had to have the guile of a Pirate Jenny then
to survive, especially as a woman. One girlfriend,
an attaché of the Brazilian consulate, smuggled
our pamphlets out in special diplomatic pouches.
The men acted as if it were good luck for women
in the Resistance to help the cause by sneaking out
the most damaging documents in our brassieres.
Once I waited it seemed all night at the train station
for my contact, the whole text rubbing its nervous
hands like an overeager boy giving me gooseflesh.
The entire newsprint issue clung so close to my
body, I'd have to scrap the hand-off completely
in an hour, the pages reduced to grapefruit pulp.
But our story would get out, I was determined,
even if I had to make a brand-new mimeograph
from an embossment of my abdomen and breasts.

Most often now I'm asked not about my own survival
or life underground, a stateless German Jew working
for the French Resistance, but about my friend,
the German Jewish philosopher Walter Benjamin,
whom I led across the Pyrenees. *Der alte Benjamin*
("Old Man Benjamin") I always called him,
even though at that time he was only forty-eight.
Now students of Benjamin, disciples of his writings—
even those who have meticulously studied my account—
still want to hear the story in my voice, as if some
detail not already pinned neatly under museum glass
might suddenly escape my memory and resurface
like the small constellations of dust here catching late
afternoon light. They want a new lens through which
another Walter Benjamin might reappear. I admit,
I've revisited this dark terrain many times to see what
I've missed, besides the one thing I might have done
to prevent Benjamin's death. Benjamin and his entourage
arrived at the border only to have their visas denied.
Had I known the already arbitrary rules had changed,
I'd have waited a day for the next arbitrary change
to reinstate what had been valid all along. Instead,
rather than return to what Benjamin had known
in the first camps, it seems he emptied a fatal dose of
morphine in a Port-Bou hotel room, under house arrest,
so that he might know the mercy of a gentler death.
Yet even the facts around his suicide are in dispute.
Documents uncovered over a decade ago in a Port-
Bou archive cast wide doubt on previous evidence.
Did Walter Benjamin commit suicide? We have reason
to view the autopsy and coroner's report with suspicion.
Now the lingering tantalizing mystery surrounding Benjamin

resides in the contents of the black briefcase he clung to
like a life preserver throughout our journey. The blackness
he clutched so firmly to his chest apparently contained
the only copy of his last manuscript. He said to me:
"It must be saved. It's more important than my life."

Doctoral students writing dissertations on
my old friend ask: "Did he say anything to you
about his manuscript? Do you know what it contained?
Do you believe that it held a new philosophy?"

ꝯ

It's easy enough to romanticize the contents
of Benjamin's black briefcase. What I recall most
about the weather-beaten bag? It had the mind
of a goat and the heft of a friar passed out on
communion wine, impervious to our best efforts
to assure its safety. I remember the black case
becoming heavier and heavier in our ascent, as if
its owner were mentally adding pages as we scaled
our way to the Spanish coast. Behind us, to the North,
la Côte Vermeille, Vermillion Coast, of Catalonia's
Roussillon, innumerable yellow-golds and reds.
I'd never seen such beauty; I gasped. It seemed
unfair to have to turn back to occupied France
while *der alte Benjamin* and his entourage departed
for what we hoped would be their lasting escape.

ꝯ

Of all the words written about Benjamin's suicide,
those I return to most are by his close friend, Brecht:

On Learning of the Suicide of the Refugee Walter Benjamin

I hear the Hand used against you, you have raised
To elude Slaughter.
Eight-years exiled, having seen the Ascent of Enemies,
Then, confronted by one impassable Boundary,
You drove yourself through one that could be crossed.

Empires crumble. The Bandit-leader
Struts about resembling a Statesman. The Peoples
No longer can see through such Armaments.
Thus the Future lies in Darkness, and the better Forces
Are weak. All this was perfectly clear to you
When you destroyed a Body capable of being tortured.

I was in my seventies when Benjamin's childhood
friend, *Gershom Scholem,* called from Jerusalem
to speak of him. I conveyed the genuine intensity
of my condolences. Then, reaching out to Scholem
in a lighter tone, said "at least the black suitcase's
contents made it to safety." Then silence.

"The manuscript," he said, "does *not* exist."
Then: "To this day, no one knows its whereabouts.
Please. You must tell me everything you know—
the manuscript must be found!" He continued,
undeterred, but all I heard was:
                    ". . . the manuscript has vanished."

And all those years I'd thought it'd been rescued.

At the age of seventy-three, I went back to Port-Bou,
Figueras, Barcelona for the first time in decades
to search for the black case and its lost contents.
The death registry lists as Benjamin's last possessions:
a brown pipe, gold pocket-watch, spectacles (red rims),
six photographs, various letters and postcards (received
and unsent), three silver fountain pens, red Florentine
stationery, enough money for Benjamin's travel companions
to pay the hotelier for his one night of house arrest,
but not enough to afford Benjamin a proper burial.
Among various personal effects, Spanish authorities note
"also a disheveled paper mass of indeterminate content."
Some suggest the papers were kept sealed up in darkness
till they were found "vermin soiled" and discarded.

Faut se débrouiller. First, you must know how
to help yourself—how to carve your own path
out of the nightmare, if you are going to survive.
You have to train yourself like a magician to
disappear and reappear, as through a needle's eye,
threading yourself invisibly through loopholes,
like weeds in sidewalk cracks, stretching impossibly
and imperceptibly through walled battlements,
using every trick and stratagem to help yourself.

Walter Benjamin may have been no *débrouillard.*
But he knew enough to help himself disappear.
The workers on his life continue. The shadows
cast by his lost opus loom so much larger now.
They carve their own path out of the nightmare.

Sometimes my memory puzzles me. It conjures
a red blouse on a clothesline, opening in the wind.
The fluted, Corinthian columns of the arms come alive
        like a sleepwalker almost waking
from an unbearable dream. The breeze breathes through
        the well-worn, translucent satin,
flexing and releasing.

Red, the far left edge of the visible color spectrum,
        the chroma closest to the infra-frequencies,
the harmonies below those we perceive;
red, the copper filaments in lightbulbs turned on and warming up;
red, the girl I was walking confidently between two rows of
Brownshirts who shouted: "Don't shop here!"
        outside a Jewish haberdashery;
red, me walking up the stairs to their threats, despite the man
        leaning into me, saying "Have you lost your mind?"—

Red, the figure in the window, fidgety now,
        behind a star of David written in smeared eggs;
and red, the feeling on my bare neck as I enter, the door
        jangling open then closed, the shopkeeper's saying:
"You should have walked away!"
and red, my knowing this, red, still needing to show him
        he's not alone; red, telling him I have no money
for a hat and red me telling him my hat size;
red, the protégé bringing hats in so many beautiful shapes;
red, his telling me the one that he likes best, the one I love
        the most but can't afford; and red, him telling me to
take the hat "Please!" I can pay him when I can, or not;
and red, me thanking him and walking out the door.

Red, the color of my hat but also the way my walking
        with it through the raging Brownshirts still causes
them to part around me like the Red Sea;
and red, how I, Lisa Fittko, a German Jew living underground
        in France, a citizen of no country, *une sale boche*,
nevertheless, could lead over a hundred exiles
like myself across the Pyrenees to safety;
I, Lisa Fittko—one person, one life—could help set another
        world within our world in motion.

III

From Three Words of a Magnetic Poetry Set
Found Caked in Dirt Beneath James Merrill's
Last Refrigerator

* Crimson * Ring * Touch *

It's true, there is no substitute for touch,
for the kiss that sets a world in motion.
One caress is all it takes, watch any nurse
in a delivery ward, each warm fingerprint

is gift. Whole histories of the heart
could be devoted to what passes
in an instant, from the snow of old skin
tumbling like dazed moths in a blizzard

of sunlight to what turns crimson
when the lit red fuse passes from lip
to tongue in a kiss first registered
as shock then recognized, taken in—

*in*seen. As when your true love
says, "Your lips—a kissable music,"
before nodding off. Leaving your mouth,
that inflamed ripe monogram of O,

an unkissed wish, that tremor
in your bones, restored. The residue
of touch, the lipstick crimson rings—
a nutrient set spreading in an instant.

Or at the promise of the touch to come,
a single note struck in the choir of itself,
when made to sing in us, is madrigal—
a resonance of every clear perception

of the world, even disappointment,
which might otherwise make for
a language cacophonous. But when
such sound takes residence in us,

the resonance instead becomes the love
we can do least without, the color of
a tapped black note, a surface shaped in
pressure—fissure, fault—of pigment, ink—

a single stroke, hoisted in the rafters of the mind;
which is just another way to know the origin
of touch as curative. (Being a little "touched"
is unavoidable.) But like a constellation

reflected perfectly then blurred in a wading pool
stirred by hand, the silver rings turn crimson
in a heart exposed, as if by touch alone, one
person, one life, might keep the world in motion.

Svendborg Sound

1. Ramsløg (Allium Ursinum)

All May, and everywhere
    the scent
of scallions seeps in from

    the shadows
wherever the Baltic salts
    the open air

in breezy atmosphere appear
    these thigh-
high, earth-grown, earthbound

    constellations:—
white popcorn clusters bursting
    at the ends of

long green reedy shafts, now lit
    hand-held
sparklers, now shooting stars.

    Or frozen
meteor showers in seemingly
    endless rows

of shadowy bouquets, these
    sweetly
pungent edible wildflowers.

2.

Late June
when Denmark's surrounding waters
warm, so

will return the transparent iridescent
swarms
of jellyfish that float along the docks

and wash
ashore each year. I could watch them
for hours

these brilliant see-through negligees
unfurling
condoms catching light and rainbows

in the bilge
of moored motor boats bobbing
up and down;

at first they seem pure contaminant:
garbage bags
misused, made only to be discarded:

aimless,
transitory, containing nothing and
nothing

themselves; but look close: see one
    open
then pulse, all waking eye. And there

    you are
—another waking I.

Mushroom Picking

The bus to Oświęcim stops first
outside the medieval city, Kraków:
the Vistula River behind us blurs
then stretches Wawel Castle's
sunstruck spires. I'm not from here,
though I chase this landscape's
incessant shadows and silences.
My Polish friend and guide—
a librarian at *Bibliotecka Jagiellonian*
raised by her grandparents to
climb the narrowest limbs in
their countryside cherry orchard—
now rising, says: "This is our *stoppe!*"
We step out into early autumn air:
cold, wet, but bright. A three-legged
dog hobbles by as we enter the dark
forest.
　　　　Along one fallen tree limb—
a shrunken arm, mummified black
partly sheathed in a gray fraying
weather-beaten sleeve of bark
now purling with crescent moons
of buckling Us and Cs edged in
medals of pale gray-blue lichen—
we see six rain-flecked white skullcaps,
now bruising orange and lilac-blue,
protruding from the earth on stems
neon-red-pink as rhubarb, the skullcaps
in dust tangles of cobwebs filled with
pencil shavings smelling more of
earth and fresh ground cinnamon.
Slimy fist-sized opalescent pearls
mimic the *amanita* local baristas mince

into ham cubes and scrape onto side-
serving plates with saucer-spills of
last night's beer to kill the summer flies.
"I *know* this one!" Basha says.
". . . But we do not gather it."
In her forest, the children choose
the largest—puff balls—to jump
on, to make mist. Basha points to a
branch, thigh-thick, where lightning
or a misdirected ax or bullet
has exposed space enough for fresh
bright blisters of yellow cauliflower
florets edged in purple and red. "It's
OK," Basha says. "But not *special.*"

Ahead, in a moldy patch of gold-yellow
leaves, we meet an older man
in sky blue overalls encrusted
with a dirt so thick and powdery,
tilted columns of light he stands in
seem to billow with smoke.
He speaks, gesturing with a butter knife
now glinting. Basha translates.

He's seen the book I carry
and people gathering perfectly
tasteless mushrooms with it.
With his other hand, he raises
a rain-dappled plastic bag steamed
up from inside with what might be
rain-flushed snails still breathing.
Or thumb-sized doorknobs
on the ends of pinky-thick

anemones. "*Opienki*," Basha says.
"*—Not in your book*, he says!
'Around the stump', it means."
(Later, online, I'll find *Armillaria
mellea*—"the honey mushroom,"
a bioluminescent.)
                    Still holding
the butter knife, the man taps at the air
above our heads, toward something
behind us, kicked up in our wake.
We turn to face a distant hillside—
a moldy white-yellow quilt
that catches light, like a stream
filling up with coins. Or a painted
antique door that might open inward
to the silent and unseen.

To Grow

(*After Piet Hein*)

There appeared before our eyes a tuft of grass
    on the earth.
Warm sunlight spread over it, as from spilled juice.
    Whatever the sunlight touches grows.

It grows in sunlight, in sudden rains, in snow squalls,
    in thunderstorms.
Every little random treat, trinket, arbitrarily given sign
    gives it form.

Small charred bits from bonfires comingling in the air with
    compromised juices,
squeezed liquids, nectars, coming going through it bloom
    fresh airs and scents.

Another world appears out of the merest discarded gloom:
    an inviting bath
edged with green waist-high spearhead corn-silk stalks tipped
    with shriner's plumes.

Even the hardest shell will stretch, the Absolute bursting
    the encasings of seeds.
Small hardly noticeable things, that weren't there before,
    now will poke through.

Softly created veins branch, leaf by leaf, into nervous systems
    out of mud.
Such fullness! And out of what? Nothing? . . . Yet it happens.
    Minute tremors,

minute spasms, minute fissures, minute breaks, minute wounds,
    minute somersaults.
Out of shadow a newly awakening world rubs its eyes, waking,
    it eclipses the sun.

We have some serious work ahead of us, without a doubt,
    we do.
One needs to believe oneself so deserving, so rich, so strong:
    To grow.

Grappa

At the cool, wet, red-amber sunset edge
     of the zinc bar, he rests a lanky arm—

his lean long hands fitful as squirrels contemplating
     flight as he explains what he's just done:

Ordered us the drink that comes from "pomace,"
     everything that even the worst winemakers

discard. Condensed assemblies of undesirables:
     pruned skins, crushed stems, bitter

seeds, dregs & detritus. I'm not from this city.
     Yet find myself entertaining a friend

from out-of-town, a former army brat, who grew
     up here in Tennessee. Mid-January, we're

three & a half hours by car from the infamous
     Lorraine Motel. Today Dr. King would

have been eighty. So we drink to him. My friend
     has the air of someone who's been walking

daily among mountains that disappear & reappear
     in low-flying clouds. He's just a little bit

taller now than the rest of us, & he seems to keep
     opening a path behind him that one might

follow inside the darkness he stands in. I imitate him
     & drink—my head snaps back then forward—

my whole body clenching around that cold burn.
        It's like trying to take in all of winter

in one breath. The empty shot glass now smells
        vaguely of green antifreeze, old toothpicks,

& our fathers' fathers' aftershave. For a moment
        I can hardly contain how much I miss my dead.

Craig Arnold, who will be dead in six months, now
        wants to tell me about his late teacher,

Larry Levis, whose place he rented in Salt Lake City.
        Larry came back a month early from his leave

like a ghost escaping Paradise, returning for everything
        the dead might come to miss. Some nights

Craig would hear a knock late at his door. Then
        a "Sorry to bother you" & "your light was on."

(It always was!) Some nights Larry came by for a smoke.
        But once it was to share something he'd been

saving for an occasion: the grappa he so loved.
        Which we drink at this Nashville zinc bar.

Larry Levis grew up in California on a vineyard
        that yielded grapes worthless for wine.

His father could only harvest them for raisins. All
        those gorgeous acres in the San Joaquin

Valley, a landscape to rival Lorca's lemon, orange,
      & almond groves. His father would have

made a killing if he'd made grappa—the thought
      never occurred to him, Levis said.

"Bottoms up," Craig says, as if standing at the edge
      of a brilliant expanse. They're all gone

now, no more solid than the words I keep laying
      out for them like breadcrumbs by which

the dead might return to us as birds from the present
      heights they currently circle & dwell in. Now,

over a year after his death, I still picture Craig there
      bracing himself for a summit that one of us

must keep climbing, the pink & green neon flashes
      refracting in the empty shot glass he holds

up to his face like a prism he just keeps turning,
      a mirror of spun starlight in his hands, as if

to say: "See this?" (the emptiness bright as a diamond,
      which blinds me) "What will you make of it?"

Fessing Up

I went to Chicago once, but I didn't inhale.
Once I was writing a song with a friend
in a dormitory when a gardener walked up
to an open window and said, What you boys
need there is a minor chord. Of course
I breathed in Illinois; I watched my breath
materialize and disappear like little tempests
that consider themselves out of existence,
but I didn't really take it in. Sure
there was the man whose car stopped
in front of us on the snowy on-ramp.
A Schlitz can fell out the door, rolled half a foot
onto the highway, then breezed beneath his car.
"Poquita gas, poquita gasoline?" he pleaded,
banging on the frosted glass with a crumpled twenty.
How could I tell him I was from out of town,
that I have no sense of direction
and couldn't return to this exact spot
even if the survival of the species depended on it.
We didn't even share a language. Not really.
I only know enough Spanish to go to the bathroom.
My Greek is good enough to get me slapped.
In English, like you, I know too much.
When the gardener walked up to the window
his tanned skin broke into a smile
and he told us he wrote music.
Do you ever wonder how many others
like him are out there making music
that no one ever hears? I could go on like this
for days if friends weren't so kindly interrupting me
with letters and phone calls. Sometimes I walk
for miles to hear the Slavic woman play the accordion.

I stand beneath her open window where she practices
and swoon to myself. I wonder if she knows
how many of us come here each day by ourselves
just to listen?

IV

A Map of the Lost World

꒳

One theme persists (from the Talmud):
To save one life is as if one saved
The entire world. For long afternoons

In Ohio, I and my ninety-year-old friend
Sat knee to knee at his kitchen table
Beneath the ceiling's bright overhead;

Between us, the map of his besieged
City, Warsaw, unfolded, unfolding
Further as he led us down streets

That no longer exist, through sewers
He knew by heart and waded those
First days of the last ghetto uprising,

Two shadows moving under boulevard,
Avenue, *ulica* (street)—the snowy dust
Now lighting up around him and us

In the refrigerator hum—a small universe
In which the Warsaw Ghetto comes
To life, stirred by his fingertips.

꒳

DC Spring. The cherry blossoms sway
Eerily outside the Museum of Remembrance,
Red-white explosions against navy-blue sky

Blackening: another inscrutable portent
Of early spring. In less than three months
The museum theater's "world premiere"

Of *Anne and Emmett*[1] will be postponed
Indefinitely after a WWII vet (ex-navy,
PT boat officer) enters the museum lobby—

Setting off the alarm—and shoots to death
A museum guard.[2] Later, in his Annapolis home,
Feds find his weapons cache and oil paints.

ॐ

Once inside, the Museum of Remembrance
Archivist leads me through the new display:
"The Well-Kept Secrets of Bad[3] Arolsen"—

Five of eleven yellowing snakeskin miles
Of moldy Nazi documents just released for
Research after seven decades. (How long it takes

To unfurl one scroll of History.) I'm here
Following a paper trail for my Ohio friend,
Now failing—whose name in Aramaic means

Heart-wise and praise (= T.)—a Shoah survivor
And widower still hoping to learn the fates
Of prison friends, when out of deep-sea digital

Memory surfaces the yellowing SS file on him.
From Dachau (one of seven internment camps
He managed to withstand) filled out in longhand

---

1 An imagined conversation between Anne Frank and Emmett Till.
2 Stephen Tyrone Johns (October 4, 1969–June 10, 2009), an African
   American ex-marine and the Holocaust Museum security guard shot to
   death shortly after opening the front door for an eighty-nine-year old
   self-professed "white supremacist."
3 German for "spa town."

And blue ink. A bottom line like a black corkscrew
Curl pulled tight by *Name der Ehefrau* (Wife) says:
Gabriella—*Gabriella?* But his late wife was *Ewa.*

And a room long-dressed in shadows now opens.

ᴣ

That March night, outside the DC hotel: lit
Monuments, a waning moon, and shooting stars
Of neon pink and green bar light below me
Blur on wet concrete; the drenched red-white

Cherry blossoms now glisten like sapphires.
I call my friend. His voice, that old-world
Baritone—chemo-chiseled to a squeaky tenor—
An old ham radio amplifier's red needle,

Quivering. This will be our last conversation.
Too tired to speak, he says: "Cowl back
Later in thee week. And I tell you *everything!*"

—But early Sunday morning, I'll hear his daughter's

Voice, and know, before she's said a word—
Each word an X, dissolving unknown history.

ᴣ

Weeks later, a parcel arrives marked: *Priorytet.*
Return address unfamiliar, a street in WARSZAWA:
The name, a world-renowned neurosurgeon/chess champion,
And my dead friend's best friend of seven decades,

"George." Or *Jerzy* (= *J.*), whose name in Greek
Means "earth worker" and a way of training
Apprentice knights with lances. *J.*, one who
Sharpens the known edges of available thought

And earth, one who labors at his work, kneading
The soil, now helps us both to reconstruct
The scene. The envelope—that seems part
Sunflower, part fallen maple leaf—contains

A glossy portrait of the sender and his wife
On a rust-brown vinyl sofa, the man's face:
Clean-shaven, elfin, grinning beneath a thick
Low-watt shock of Einstein hair, beige shirt—

Beige sweater vest—lit by a red, white, blue
Striped bowtie. His wife of seven decades
Beside him on the couch looks uncertain:
A stark contrast to the portrait of her, hovering

Like a thought balloon above their heads
On the wood paneling. (Her younger self,
Mid-argument, looks like a cat ready to
Pounce.) In old age she only recognizes *J.*

Whose letter now begins to address
Some of what his friend no longer can.
He mentions a book, then untangles
The writer's full name—a bramble of

Polish consonants, which in Hebrew mean:
"One who delivers or rescues from oblivion":
(First name: *Moshe*, nickname: *Mietek* = *M.*).
Also meaning: "One drawn as from water"—

As if *J.*'s articulation pulled *M.* from depths
Where he long languished; or the infant Moses—
With whom *M.* shares a name—then the
Retired shaper of available thought and earth

Says: ". . . And I tell you things . . . I tell *nobody else!*"

࿊

Through adolescence, I shook a Magic
8 Ball, almost religiously, to answer
Crushed-out questions, turned my
Seedy dime-store orb till it surrendered
The answer I already knew I wanted most:
(Usually: ALL SIGNS POINT TO YES!)

Now I trawl Google (an oracle good as any)
For any clues and find the memoir: *Mietek's*
<u>A PRISONER OF HOPE</u>. Later, at home,
I flip through the university library's near-
Pristine copy, when suddenly one sentence
Unfurls, practically stampeding to life

With my dead friend's full name. Rising
In the bright dust of flickering home movie
Black-and-whites: Warsaw; October '39.
A month after Poland's invaded by Nazis.
M. is a new physician—just married—
Now an officer. His father-in-law, a WWI

Hero (cavalry—three times awarded Poland's
Purple Heart) believes *M.*'s chances of survival
Dubious at best. His evidence?:—*Moshe's* poor
Showing at playing cards: (". . . Every day,

You play worse. But today you played me, *Mietek*,
Like it was a *hundred* years from now!") The

War hero escorts his son-in-law to the Russian
Front himself, leaving the family women
Behind in Warsaw. In three months, it's toxic:
Nazis occupy the war hero's Warsaw apartment
(An SS Lieutenant Memmler and a henchman,
Who are behaving "well enough" thus far

Even bringing the women: ". . . flour, oil, sugar.
And for no fee!") Fearing good behavior won't last,
The women take the long train south ". . . to the Black
Sea." Feb. '40. All "arrive safely" at the Odessa home.
But an unexpected fourth has joined their company:
Gabriella's pre-war Warsaw boyfriend: —*Tadzik!*—

Alive again, at twenty-two, and our protagonist.

&

It all seems like doomed relations from the start:
The terms: A = 1 [cramped studio apartment];
+ [(3 couples)/(The Black Sea)] − 1 [unmarried]
+ [2 cots + 1 bed] ÷ C = [disapproval: their parents'].

All variables make for an equation—resolvable as: π.
The next eight months are a Tao of calculus ("the study
Of change") when a letter from *T.*'s father arrives
Demanding his only son return ". . . immediately!"

T. returns to Odessa ". . . multiple times"
(From Warsaw). *M.* says in mid-March *T.*'s given
". . . An ultimatum" from his mother, *Sabina*.
That night, *T.* removes himself completely from

The Black Sea board "... *never to return*." Nov. '40.
First snows, *Gabriella* gives birth—to a baby girl.

ॐ

Yet here the binding agent holding everything
In place in *Mietek's* painted landscapes—having
Spanned such distances—memory, Time-Space—
Gradually begins itself to dissolve in snowy flakes:

(But how accurate is any representation? Even
This?) By the time the Nazis invade Poland,
T.'s mother was *already dead*. And mail service
Has long ended. So who delivered these letters?

And how did they arrive? Can we know? Cut
To: The Liberation. The orrery of Love's planets
Realigns, various characters caught in its gears.

Gabriella now has another man—a trial lawyer (*Lolek*
= *L.*), also from Warsaw, Jewish, who left a wife
And daughter behind, in the Warsaw Ghetto.[4]

---

4 Meanwhile, *T.* and his father, *Henryk* (= *H.*) are also imprisoned in the
Warsaw Ghetto (with approximately 400,000 other Polish Jews). *H.*, chief
surgeon of Warsaw's Jewish Hospital at the time of the Nazi invasion of
Poland, dies in April 1941 "from a wound infection when he cuts himself
during an operation. In those pre-antibiotic days [his death] may have been
avoided if instruments could have been sterilized properly" (Charles Roland,
Courage Under Siege. Oxford University Press, 1992, pp. 85-86). After the
Warsaw Ghetto, *T.* will be sent to six other concentration camps: Treblinka,
Maidanek, Birkenau, Sachsenhausen, Dachau XI, and Dachau IV. Found
"face down in the snow" when liberated by the Allies, he weighs seventy
pounds and is "very close to death"; it will take "three months of intensive
care to keep him alive." A fellow survivor (*Ewa*) will help nurse him back to
health; they will marry in 1947 (Tadeusz Stabholz, *Siedem piekieł* [*Seven Hells*].
Specjalne wydanie czasopisma [special limited edition], Stuttgart, 1947; and
from oral testimony). Note that the dates of *Gabriella's* father's letter and other
sources of the marriage date are also in dispute.

꙳

Six months after the war, neither lover knows
How their futures will "square" with their pasts.
Cut to: Odessa Depot. Spring '45. *Gabriella's L.*

And her father board a train to search for
Survivors. A month later, a letter arrives
For *Gabriella* postmarked BERLIN. Her father,

Stacho: ". . . Dear Child, I'll not even try to describe
What I've seen. Instead, I'll come right to the point.
Two days ago I found your beloved *T.* in Germany.

At a camp in Stuttgart for the Dispossessed.
. . . He looked half-starved, confused, and not
Visibly happy at all to be seeing me. *Tadzik?* I said.

You're alive! Now you may have your *Gabriella*
And your daughter, awaiting you in the Ukraine!"

꙳

Almost the living image of a fruitless, winter
        Tree confronting a brewing, nearly human,
                Weather system—pre-storm—

So barren of affect, *T.*, *Stacho* writes, said: This is
        Most difficult to say—*especially to you*—
                But I'm *already* married.

Next day, waiting in Odessa, *Gabriella* receives
        Another letter. Postmark: WARSZAWA
                (From *L.*). She sees the long lines

For groceries outside then reads: His wife and child—
They: ". . . did *not* survive."

ॐ

Jerzy and *Mietek* speak of the same man
I write of, yet he becomes a different person
To each, taking another shape completely
Before dissolving again in smoky breath.
Cut to November '45. A letter arrives
For *Gabriella* and *L.* (now her husband)
From her father to say he's found a place

For the newlyweds "to start again"—
Seaside in Gdansk. Later (quoting *M.*):
". . . Now the couple may begin living
The lives they've wanted all along. . . ."
Then *M.* adds: ". . . *Tadzik* never sought
Out *Gabriella* or their daughter again."
"Not true!" *Jerzy* tells me by phone

And across six time zones. Once, by
Chance, after the war, *Jerzy* saw *Gabriella*
Walking along the beach (outside Gdansk,
At Sopot). She told him *Tadzik* had found
Her after the war. "But she no longer
Wanted *he-yhm*." When the Berlin Wall
Fell, their daughter found her father

Who paid her airfare, round-trip, Jerusalem
To Cleveland. Others close to her father
T. confide that they both hoped for some
Sort of "reconciliation." Then the lost
Daughter saw how fully family illness

(*Ewa's*) had ravaged most, if not all, of
His savings. She lost interest. Another

Paint fleck sparkles then crumbles to flakes.

၃၇

The Lost Cave Paintings of Grotto Cosquer

When I finally saw the museum's underwater
Footage of explorer *Henri Cosquer* in silhouette,
Backlit by bright high beams and floating

Like a cosmonaut, trailing a long black umbilicus—
And *Cosquer* at last arrives at the right opening
To find the cave paintings of *Calanque Morgiou,*

The most perfectly intact petroglyphs then known
Anywhere since Lascaux—even though the whole
Scene was staged, *Cosquer* still seemed to be entering

The lost city of Atlantis. His head poked through
The underground wading pool's surface; he stands
Waist-high inside a cavern sparkling and echoing.

He takes off his diver's mask, and tank, and rubs
A black-gloved hand along one waist-thick yellowing
Downward-spiraling fang whose lower half, submerged,

Conceals not bats or swifts but the blue-silver
Undersides of neon fish, darting in and out,
Around and through the explorer's shadowy legs.

Fish like shooting stars lighting up red and black
Images whose pigments, ground from wood
Charred black around fires where, it seems,

Our ancestors gathered and told stories
Of the day's hunt, and of their days, and ate,
Mixing the blackened wood with animal fat

Dripping from the day's kill, first on a spit
And turning; and, for pigment, adding warm
Blood, then blowing the whole conglomerate

Hot in the mouth, through hollow reeds,
Onto these walls outlined in charcoal; among
The red and black figures of aurochs, buffalo,

Seals, dolphins, jellyfish, a guide points out
The image of the hunter killed at his own hand—
By his or another's spear. Before *Henri Cosquer,*

Three other explorers died trying to find
This long unknown spot, a place for centuries
Held out of time in time. Then, for a time,

I wondered if my search would make of me
A *Cosquer* or another Ahab, destroying himself,
His men, his whole vehicle for transformation,

By making a curse of the thing he craved.

I never wanted to make of you some trick
Of mirrored light, or lie of the imagination.
I never wanted this flurry of shooting stars
To obscure your final place in the night sky.
Is this why you kept the story to yourself?
Because there was no gift in it for us?
Your silence, now absolute, is not so different
From the pauses that follow certain music.
Or what sometimes comes before the words.
That some real part of you, still vital, waiting
To be found on the map of the lost world
Might return, if I went far enough, is the stuff
Of poetry. The kind that says, Be vigilant.
We must love one another while there is time.

In today's mail arrives: a square, white bubble
Wrap mailer of Frisbee-span length and heft.
A parcel (from the Museum of Remembrance)
Nearly big enough to fill one panel of a prison-
Barred storm windowpane—suddenly flooded
By late afternoon light so blinding it turns
The breath-steamed glass white. Inside slides
Out a silver, metallic DVD diskette that grows
More rainbow-colored the more I tilt it in air;
Its contents (for another time) the enclosed
Note says: "All known Nazi files" on my friend
And his prison mates. How long will we shoulder
What we can bear of what we'll never know
Before the weight breaks us, or we grow into it?

Boundary Waters

ॐ

All along the Mediterranean Coast,
Night fishermen cast blindly into
The Sea, their lit lures neon green
And yellow helixes doubling in an

Endless, wet black mirror. Another
Exit and entrance hovers between
Worlds. All Saints'. The night before—
All Hallows'—the dinner conversation

Revolves on distances, the dead,
The creaturely, what passes for
Understanding in our world. One friend
Speaks of a place off Maui she swam

Every day alongside spinner dolphins.
Often she could hear their approach—
A sound like laughter underwater,
Nearing. They always seemed to know

To leave—before the tour boats came.
Some days you might believe the idea
Most beautiful. Someone round the table
Says sonar lets sea mammals perceive

Things we only glimpse. One dolphin
Studied in an isolation tank, *echolocating*,
Homed in on its pregnant researcher—
That day in distress—as if trying to heal

Both with steady bursts of seismic frequency.

～

Like kids who'll do anything to stay
Awake—even scare themselves—we keep
Telling each other stories, each one more
Unsettling than the next: A friend waking

At her mother's feet in the family station
Wagon, asking her parents, "Are we
Dead yet?" My first visit home from college.
Thanksgiving. The white sheets of Ohio

Snow squalls tumbling on the highway,
Swirling behind the windshield, before
Our eyes, then gone, like so many migrating
Spirits, when our northbound two-door

Pitches right, blindsided by a semi, whose
Grizzly snout shoves us the wrong way
Up I-71 for half a mile until we slide
Off, almost effortlessly, into a snowbank.

ॐ

(*Quetico*)
First island in the chain of lakes known
As "the boundary waters" (Ojibwe for:
"Spirit that resides in Beauty, wilderness"

And "in places of undisturbed Immensity").
On the Canadian side the boundary waters
Are protected; only so many travelers

May enter at a time. Days go by before
You'll find another person, though you'll
See loons, moose, grouse, snapping turtles,

And beavers, whose dams can overtake
Lakes and streams before the same
Lakes and streams eventually overtake them.

I see my father here, on the protected side,
Camping with the white wolves he never saw,
And still never sees, though they may eye

Him from afar, their gray smoky night breath
Before them, then gone, their red-amber gazes
Hot as coals reflecting fire; I see my father here,

While the black bears roam the North woods.
Once he took my brother and me in a canoe
Out on the lake before dawn, and we returned,

Content, dangling the morning's bright catch
On a stringer, only to find our rented ramshackle
Ransacked—chairs overturned, clothes strewn

In elaborate patterns of disarray. We found
The storm-cloud white Igloo container
Still reeking of skinned walleye and pike

And slimy to the touch, the ultramarine blue
Fist-thick lid still on, and clamped down tight,
But now with a whole black bear paw print

Pressed deep into the blue top's broad cheek.
The black bear will return, but only after
My father and brother and I drive away.

On the American side of *Quetico*, campers
Leave the carcasses and innards of fish
On the rocks; these meager offerings to

The lower gods ward off birds of prey.
Most gulls observe a pecking order
Unless a rogue gull appears—squawking,

Feckless, a scavenger, no doubt hunger-
Deranged. Once a large snapping turtle
Surfaced by my father's boat, the morning's

Fish still on the stringer, unable to escape.
His canoe-mate paddle-thwacked the turtle
Onto its back, but quickly it righted itself

And came at him. The men fended off
The turtle, and the other fishermen carved
Their catch, tossing the glistening innards

To the rocks. Then the lead gull swooped
Down on the fish remains and rose
Into the sky again, only to have another

Gull pursue; it dropped the fish back
Into the water. The turtle, or another,
Surfaced, took the meat, dove, then

Resurfaced; yet another gull grabbed
The fish and ascended, back to the clouds.
The other gulls now dive-bombed

The victorious gull so furiously it dropped
The fish back to the turtle, which choked
Down the remains whole and disappeared.

Twenty minutes later, there was no sign
Of them, or that anything had happened,
The water still as a figure on a printed page.

꒢

Late May in Provincetown. Kicking up
The fine sand of Hatch's Harbor. The sun
Low in the sky, a bright red blood orange,

Spreading across the waves like wildfire
And the sand reaching that red shade
When my wife turns to me from that

Immensity to ask if we have time to see
The whales. *Yes,* I say, when four car lengths
Offshore, appears—like a baby concert

Grand—a submerged piano, suddenly
Dislodged, raw umber brown, veins of
Salty freshly uncorked champagne-froth

Running down its back and sides in silver
Rivulets, a whale—shiny as a liver—
The mist of its belched wheeze breezing

Our hair over our faces—the beachcombers'
Kids now screaming: *"Do you see it? Do you
See it?"* Will it beach, betrayed by signals

We don't even know we're sending? I think.
Running now, we toss back and forth
Plans to save it, all wrong, all late; watch

It surface three more times, each closer to
Shore, before the whale heads out to open sea.
The mid-March day I learned of my friend's death

Ended with the strangest sensation. Putting
Out the light, I wondered how I'd get through
The long night. Then my lifelong fear of

The dark eased, erased, it seemed—How could
It be? Yet how could it be otherwise?—by you,
My newest friend among the gathering shades.

V

Larry Levis in Provincetown

(*June 2007*)

This is how I am summoned from nothingness:
in faded cutoffs, moonlighting at Connie's Bakery

where I keep reading Rilke to Jenny, the pastry chef,
who rolls her eyes, & blows flour into my tired face.

Beneath my limp baker's hat & stained white smock
I still wear my favorite Hawaiian shirt, the color

of bubble gum, absinthe, & night. We are permitted
to choose but one companion for the great journey,

so Garcia Lorca is here with me;—we arrived last week
as "guest worker summer help." You'll be happy

to know that our work continues, as before, in Death.
Last night we finally had that conversation about

the moon, & mirrors—why they can't tell us
everything they see. We stood at an ivy-lined gate

two summers too late to deliver Stanley Kunitz our best
vermouth & news of Roethke & the other immortal poets

whose ranks by now, at long last, he's joined. Instead,
our poet of black notes took off his white tuxedo shirt

&, facing Stanley's last masterpiece—his front yard
garden, which still revises itself in preparation

for his return—Garcia Lorca revealed thumb-sized
lavender crescent moons, the eerie constellation

across his chest above the heart, the scars of bullet holes
from Franco's *Guardia Civil*; he told me everything—

from the faces of the firing squad to digging his own grave.
He says the landscape of his dreams has already drifted

from the Alhambra's gardens, wading pools, & almond groves
to the salt marsh at Black Fish Creek & the starlit wisteria

he affectionately calls: "These endlessly creeping vines
of strumpet braids!" And the delicate braids of challah

we braid each day rise like old lovers awakening to our touch
restored. You should see the lean, aristocratic

hands of Garcia Lorca—they've never been so strong!
I didn't think such mortal progress was still possible for us.

Or that I would again be permitted access to the knowledge
that comes in a love amplified by the stirrings of the world.

And then I recognized something in the insistent, winding
taproot of an oak, which pierced me with the recognition

that is holy, & I felt the tug of gravity's widening spell.
So that even if Garcia Lorca & I are just scraping by

with all the others working for peanuts in high season,
to be alive again & living in a hot seaside town

is good as any afterlife
& probably our best chance at happiness.

"Missoula Eclipse" is written in the voice of Richard Hugo (December 21, 1923–October 22, 1982), a celebrated American poet who taught for many years at the University of Montana and wrote poems that simultaneously praised and lamented the lives of abandoned towns, landscapes, and, especially, people of the Pacific Northwest. He met and befriended the poet James Wright (December 13, 1927–March 25, 1980) while both were Theodore Roethke's students at the University of Washington. Richard Hugo's *The Real West Marginal Way* (particularly his essay on Wright) was extremely helpful in the writing of this poem.

"Nights & Days of 2007: Autumn" was initially drafted in the Water Street apartment (in Stonington, CT) of the late poet James Merrill (March 3, 1926–February 6, 1995); in this apartment one of the "leading poets of his generation" surprised many of his longtime readers when he temporarily turned away from his "chronicles of love and loss" to write (with the help of a Ouija board) the epic poem *The Changing Light at Sandover*, which would garner many of the most distinguished prizes available to an American poet.

"The Red Scarf & the Black Briefcase" is written in the voice of Lisa Fittko (August 23, 1909–March 12, 2005) born "Elisabeth Eckstein" in Uzhgorod, a small town on the eastern border of the Austrian-Hungarian Monarchy that became part of the Soviet Union after World War II (now part of Ukraine). Most of the significant details in the poem have been adapted from Fittko's two memoirs: *Solidarity and Treason* and *Escape through the Pyrenees* (both published by Northwestern University Press). Politically active most of her life, she grew up in Germany and, during WWII, fled to France where, after her own incarceration, she fought in the resistance. In what may be the most noted event of her second book, the first person she led across the Pyrenees was the now much-celebrated German Jewish philosopher and literary critic Walter Benjamin (July 15, 1892–September 30, 1940). Despite many physical obstacles, including treacherous terrain and

Benjamin's poor health, she successfully led him across the Pyrenees to the border of Spain, where, shortly after they parted ways, Spanish authorities arrested him. The details of his death—an apparent suicide by morphine overdose—remain a mystery. Apparently the guards threatened to deport him to France, where he was sure to be sent to a concentration camp. (He'd already been imprisoned in one of the first French concentration camps—at Vernuche.) His body was found the next morning. This loss (which the great German poet and playwright Bertolt Brecht would call "the first real blow that Hitler had dealt German letters") may not have been entirely in vain, for shortly after discovering Benjamin's remains, the guards that detained him reopened the Spanish border to German refugees, including those arrested with him.

"Svendborg Sound": Though recent guidebooks may say "there is no reason to spend even a night in Svendborg," Bertolt Brecht lived there with his family from 1933–1939, when first exiled from Hitler's Germany; his friend Walter Benjamin visited him there frequently, particularly in the summers of '34, '36, and '38. At one point, Benjamin's now famous "lost library" was in Svendborg (Brecht even used it—or tried to—in letters to lure others to visit him in what he called "Danish Siberia"). Ramsløg blooms in May to early June, when Benjamin usually met up with Brecht. Here, Brecht wrote many of the works for which he is most known, including *Galileo* and *Mother Courage*.

"Grappa": Craig Arnold (November 16, 1967–c. April 27, 2009), one of the most promising and accomplished poets of his generation, was lost on the small volcanic island of Kuchinoerabujima, Japan, on or around April 27, 2009, after failing to return from an evening hike alone to explore an active volcano. While Japanese law mandates that government-backed searches last for three days, on April 30, 2009, the Japanese government agreed to extend the search an additional three days after a resounding public outcry (registered and made possible, oddly if expediently enough, by the then relatively new social networking website Facebook and a page called "Find Craig Arnold," constructed nearly overnight to spread the word of his disappearance and post updates on the search). A trail of footprints believed to be Arnold's were last spotted near a high cliff, where he is thought to have fallen fatally some time near the date of his disappearance. His remains were never found.

Larry Levis (September 30, 1946–May 8, 1996) grew up in California's San Joaquin Valley and would come to write what poet Robert Mezey called a poetry fueled by "the nourishing shock of fresh ideas that rise from the work of the true poet." A recipient of numerous awards for poems that would define a late twentieth-century high-water mark for the meditative lyric, Levis would die of a heart attack just shy of his fiftieth birthday.

"Larry Levis in Provincetown": Federico García Lorca (June 5, 1898– c. August 12/13, 1936) is regarded by many as "the most important Spanish poet and dramatist of the twentieth century." In 1936, he was arrested by Falangists, and after a few days in prison he "disappeared." Though stories of Lorca's violent torture and murder surfaced almost immediately after his disappearance, his remains were never found. Now, more than seventy-five years after Lorca's disappearance, experts have yet to find—or determine the whereabouts of—his remains.

ACKNOWLEDGMENTS

My heartfelt thanks go out to all of the following editors who published these poems, sometimes in earlier versions:
Blackbird: "From Three Words of a Magnetic Poetry Set Found Caked in Dirt Beneath James Merrill's Last Refrigerator"; *Columbia Magazine*: "Larry Levis in Provincetown"; *Columbia Poetry Review* (Chicago): "Missoula Eclipse"; *From Bodhgaya to the Cuyahoga: Creative & Intellectual Expressions of Spiritual Culture*: "Boundary Waters"; *5 AM*: "Mushroom Picking"; *The Hudson Review*: "Nights & Days of 2007: Autumn"; *Michigan Quarterly Review*: "A Map of the Lost World"; *The New Republic*: "Fessing Up"; *New South*: "Grappa"; *Salt Hill Journal*: "Svendborg Sound"; *Southeast Review*: "The Red Scarf & the Black Briefcase."

"Missoula Eclipse" also appeared in *From the Other World: Poems in Memory of James Wright*, edited by Bruce Henrickson (Lost Hills Books); and in *Chautauqua Literary Review: Faculty Issue* (reprinted with permission).

"To Grow" and "Larry Levis in Provincetown" also appeared in *Fog and Woodsmoke: Behind the Image*, edited by Stephani Schaefer (Lost Hills Books).

"Nights & Days of 2007: Autumn" also appeared in *The Southeast Review* and on the James Merrill House website (http://www.james merrillhouse.org/writer_Rick_Hilles_p1.html); it was also nominated for a 2011 Pushcart Prize.

"The Red Scarf & the Black Briefcase" was performed (with musical interludes) at the Camargo Foundation's *la Batterie* (Cassis, France) as part of *Cabaret Ambulant a Camargo "Les Mondes perdus"* on December 9, 2009, with Kimberly Jannarone as Lisa Fittko and Kate Soper singing and playing on the piano songs by Brecht, Weill, and Purcell. The piece was performed again with the original cast on

March 19, 2010, at the Wyatt Center Rotunda on the Peabody campus of Vanderbilt University, thanks to the generous support of the following: Jay Clayton and Mark Jarman of the Department of English and Creative Writing; Leah Marcus and the Program in Jewish Studies; Mona Frederick and the Robert Penn Warren Center; Helmut Smith and the Max Kade Center for European and Germanic Studies; Liz Lunbeck and the Department of History; Michael A. Rose and Amy Jarman of the Blair School of Music; Jen Holt and the Writing Studio; Lynn Ramey and Virginia Scott of French and Italian; Barbara Hahn and Germanic and Slavic Languages; Terryl Hallquist and the Theater Department; Teresa Goddu and American Studies; Kimberly Bess of Peabody College; Ellen B. Goldring of Peabody's Department of Leadership, Policy and Organization; and Chancellor Nicholas S. Zeppos and Lydia A. Howarth. Special thanks also go to Margaret Quigley, Janis May, Kate Daniels, Connie Higginson and Leon Selig (of the Camargo Foundation), Ruth Smith, Zachery Asher (Greenberg), Kendra De Colo, Lisa Dordal, Mindy Bell, Madeleine Fentress, and Andrew Rahal. My deepest thanks to everyone who helped make these performances possible.

I also want to thank the Mrs. Giles Whiting Foundation for a Whiting Writers' Award; Vanderbilt University, for its generous support, most recently in the form of a Mellon Faculty Development Award; the American Academy in Rome; the Brecht House (Svendborg, Denmark); the Camargo Foundation (Cassis, France); the Ragdale Foundation (Lake Forest, IL); the Ledig House (Ghent, NY); Blue Mountain Center (Blue Mountain, NY); the Spiro Arts Center in Park City, Utah; the Stonington Village Improvement Association; and the James Merrill House Committee for providing the ideal circumstances for many of these poems to come into being.

And with special thanks to Mark Jarman, Kate Daniels, Grace Schulman, Ed Ochester, Glenn Kurtz, and especially to Nancy Reisman.